THE WITCH AND THE HYSTERIC

THE WITCH AND THE HYSTERIC

THE MONSTROUS MEDIEVAL IN
BENJAMIN CHRISTENSEN'S *Häxan*

Alexander Doty† and Patricia Clare Ingham

dead letter office

BABEL Working Group

punctum books ∗ brooklyn, ny

THE WITCH AND THE HYSTERIC: THE MONSTROUS
MEDIEVAL IN BENJAMIN CHRISTENSEN'S *HÄXAN*
© Alexander Doty and Patricia Clare Ingham, 2014

First published in 2014 by
dead letter office, BABEL Working Group
an imprint of punctum books
Brooklyn, New York
http://punctumbooks.com

The BABEL Working Group is a collective and desir-
ing-assemblage of scholar-gypsies with no leaders or followers, no top and no bottom, and only a middle. BA-
BEL roams and stalks the ruins of the post-historical
university as a multiplicity, a pack, looking for other roaming
packs with which to cohabit and build temporary shelters
for intellectual vagabonds. We also take in strays.

ISBN-13: 978-0692230152
ISBN-10: 0692230157

Cover Image: still-frame from *Häxan*, dir. Benjamin
Christensen (Svensk Filmindustri, 1922 / Criterion Collection, 2001).

TABLE OF CONTENTS

Dedicated, with love, to the memory of
Alexander Michael Doty, 1954-2012

Sometime during the fall of 2000, at an English Department faculty retreat at Lehigh University in Bethlehem, PA, Alex Doty and I cooked up our somewhat wacky project, "The Monstrous and the Medieval." We inaugurated the project with a team-taught course (held during the spring semester of 2001) that paired premodern texts (mostly literary) with relevant films. It was during this class that Alex introduced me to Benjamin Christensen's *Häxan*, and that I insisted he read the *Malleus Maleficarum*. From that pairing, and the ensuing conversations, the idea for this book was hatched. We published our first collaborative essay in 2003, a co-authored piece on Val Tournier's film, *Cat People*. Alex pursued his intellectual pleasures with brio—and his clear enjoyment gave me (at the time recently tenured and so overly serious and exhausted) a new lease on thinking, and a larger sense of the possibilities for style and substance in my writing.

Life intervened in ways that made our collaboration a bit more irregular. I moved to Bloomington in 2003, though we continued our work: during Alex's regular visits, or on occasions when I could make it to the Lehigh Valley. When Alex himself moved to Bloomington in 2008, we rediscovered the impetus to get back to the book. In the Spring of 2012, we reconvened and decided that our reading of *Häxan* was long enough, and layered enough, to be a short book. In early summer we submitted it for consideration for inclusion in punctum books' new (and fabulous) list. We had hopes that this would revive the larger book project, and looked forward to more collaboration.

We never got the chance. Alex's untimely death, in August 2012, cut short a brilliant and dynamic career. His loss has touched so many, in so many ways. Just two weeks after he died, we received the readers' reports from punctum, including recommendations for revision, and a green light for publication. The subsequent revisions have been slow, but Alex's voice has been in my ear, his notes on pages before me, and in a treasured archive of our email exchanges preserved in his files and given to me by his family after his death.

Spending the last several months with Alex in my heart, and head, and on the pages around me has been moving and difficult, wonderful, inspiring, and at times overwhelming. I know these revisions would have been wittier had he been here—but I hope that some of his spirit and tone has made it into the work that follows. Irreverent and edgy; compassionate and hilarious; brave and understated, his voice was one of a kind. I am so grateful that his one-of-a-kind voice lingers. I am a better scholar, a better teacher, a better writer because Alex Doty was my collaborator. But because Alex Doty was my friend, I have laughed more, traveled more, walked more, admired more old buildings and cemeteries, I've gone to more musicals, and plays, more films, art museums, concerts, and drag shows. I know the porn-star names of many of my closest friends. I've had more dark chocolate, fresh blueberries, and pumpkin, and really, really, really excellent Tequila.

ACKNOWLEDGEMENTS

Special Thanks for encouragement and support to, Judith Brown, D. Rae Greiner, Corey Creekmur, Ben Santa Maria, Bob Jacobs and Dave Artman, Rosemary and Bob Mundhenk, Shane Vogel, Beth Dolan, and Emma Dolan Kautz.

Thanks to Barb Klinger for comments on an earlier draft, and to the two anonymous readers for punctum books for their expert guidance. Publisher, Editor, and all around force of nature, Eileen Joy has been encouraging and understanding in equal measure. I am grateful to her for helping me get this into print, and also to her editorial assistant on our book, Emily Russell.

Doug Moore held my hand the whole time.

ᴐ— INTRODUCTION

Benjamin Christensen's Swedish/Danish film *Häxan* (known under its English title as *Witchcraft Through the Ages*) has entranced, entertained, shocked, and puzzled audiences for nearly a century. First premiered in late 1922, the elaborately staged and produced 108-minute production holds the title as the most expensive Scandinavian silent film in history. Interest in *Häxan* has endured well beyond the silent era: it was re-released in 1941 in Denmark with newly-edited intertitles, and including an extended documentary introduction starring Christensen himself; the film would be released yet again in 1968 (this time in an abbreviated 77-minute format) as an avantgarde event, featuring dramatic narration by Beat Generation icon, William S. Burroughs, and an eclectic jazz score. In 2001, *Häxan* appeared in a DVD edition as part of *The Criterion Collection*, including both a fully-restored print of the original film and Burroughs' shorter 1968 version, and featuring extensive production notes and commentary by Danish film scholar Casper Tybjerg. New soundtracks for the original silent version continue to be imagined, most recently in 2010.[1]

---

[1] For an account of the history of film scores, see Gillian Anderson, "About the Music," in the 2001 Criterion DVD booklet.

Häxan, it seems, won't quite let its audiences go. Yet despite this impressive production history, Christensen's film has received relatively little critical commentary. Scholars have noted Christensen's influence on 20th-century filmmakers Luis Brunel and Val Lewton; and critics have described the film's surrealism as well as its "audacious theatricality," as entrancing in the psychedelic 1960s, becoming, as Mark Bourne puts it, "the *Reefer Madness* of devil-worshipping witchcraft movies."[2] Yet no one has yet explained the film's uncanny mix of documentary and fantasy, history and theatrics, or queried its odd juxtaposition of religion and science, its irreverent mixing of the distant past and contemporary culture. The film's uncanny content is compounded by its formal strangeness, a mixture of quasi-documentary with fictional episodes, illustrated lectures alongside docudrama recreations and dreamscapes. Is this a documentary, a horror flick, or both?

Organized into seven "chapters" of varying length, *Häxan* begins with a formal lecture and filmic slide show purporting to narrate the history of demonic belief through the ages. The opening tracks belief in the devil as a primitive instinct, a version of pre-scientific error and superstition in a lecture illustrated via woodcuts and artistic renderings of worldviews dating from ancient times. Chapter 2 offers, in contrast to the documentary tenor of the preceding section, a series of short dramatic recreations, episodes dramatizing "medieval" belief in witches, or dreamscapes visualizing the devil's seductive attractions. The third chapter—the longest focalized narrative in the entire film—relates the story of a woman unjustly accused of witchcraft and tortured by the hierarchy of the medieval Catholic Church. Chapters 4 and 5 depict aspects of

---

[2] On these points, see Mark Bourne's review, "Häxan/ Witchcraft Through the Ages: The Criterion Collection," *The DVD Journal* [n.d.]: http://www.dvdjournal.com/reviews/h/haxan_cc.shtml.

witchcraft trials and practices of torture, showing precise details of torture devices and their use. Chapter 6 returns to the non-narrative form of the opening to show a range of related delusions or perversions as contributing phenomena. And, suddenly, with the seventh and final section, titled "1921," the film leap-frogs over four centuries of history to the time contemporary with the film's original release. This final section repeatedly cross-cuts the "medieval" witch and the "modern" hysteric, highlighting diverse commonalities as well as differences between "then" and "now."

Christensen offers a complex view of the medieval era as deeply entwined with monstrous imaginings, and Christensen's *häxan* (the Swedish word for *witch*) is, we will argue, a monstrously medieval figure. Yet if, throughout *Häxan*, the film juxtaposes medieval witches with modern women, it is neither entirely consistent nor entirely clear precisely what this means. Nor are *Häxan*'s historical temporalities secure. Christensen's film is, paradoxically, both chronologically specific and anachronistically out-of-joint. Intertitles emphasize the witch as an unrelentingly medieval phenomenon ("Such were the Middle Ages," claims one early on, "when witchcraft and the devil's work were sought everywhere"). Yet the film's recreations of particular episodes are strangely specified as to date, and associated with a later (arguably post-medieval) time: the first fictional reenactment (in the film's second part) identifies the setting as the "Home of a Sorceress," circa "A.D. 1488" (i.e., an early modern time). Particular witchy figures, furthermore, generate wildly ambiguous representational effects in similarly confused terms: *Häxan*'s medieval witches include "mad" nuns, homeless widows, eroticized seductresses, and Karna, the "sorceress" given to dispensing apparently reliable love potions. In a final sequence of film dissolves, Christensen compares and contrasts these "medieval" women with a series of modern ones. The latter group is eclectic, and includes an aviatrix, old and poor women, actresses, pyromaniacs, professional women, and well-to-do hysterics

What are we to make of the unsettling effect of *Häxan's* associations of "medieval" and "modern" women alongside the film's startling elision of four centuries of European history? Christiansen's juxtaposition of past and present, of the history of modern women via the tribulations of the monstrous witch, is provocative and puzzling in equal measure. In this chapbook, we suggest that the puzzle of Christensen's *Häxan* might be unraveled by attending to the film's provocative and paradoxical medievalism, its fantasy of the Middle Ages. We argue here that understanding Christensen's medievalism is crucial to understanding the politics of gender and culture with which *Häxan* is preoccupied.

As one might expect, *Häxan's* medievalism, like its representational politics, seems confused. What is clear, however, is that in developing *Häxan*, Christensen was influenced by the collocation of various texts about witches, including an infamous fifteenth-century manual for witch hunters, as well as by early twentieth-century developments in psychiatry and psychoanalysis. Christensen was not the only prominent modern thinker to consult the premodern history of witchcraft in a narrative aimed at the modern female subject. Just over twenty years before *Häxan* was released, no less a luminary than Sigmund Freud would cite the medieval witch as crucial to the "prehistory" of his controversial work on hysteria.[3] The work to which Freud referred was Heinrich Kramer's infamous 1486 handbook for witch hunters, *Malleus Maleficarum*, the text that Christensen claimed inspired his work as

---

[3] Sigmund Freud, "The Aetiology of Hysteria" (1896), in James Strachey, ed. and trans., *The Standard Edition of the Complete Psychological Works of Sigmund Freud*, Vol. 3 (London: Hogarth Press, 1962), 189–221.

well.[4] Associations between witchcraft and hysteria were promoted by figures like Jean Martin Charcot, Josef Breuer, and their followers, Freud and Pierre Janet—all of whom drew upon medieval and early modern witch hunting in constructing theories about women's mental problems, especially hysteria. This psychiatric yoking of the medieval and the modern as it concerned women's lives and subjectivities seems the most likely source for *Häxan*'s striking form.

By his own report, Christensen's accidental discovery of a copy of Kramer's work in a used bookstore provided the catalyst for his innovative film. When Christensen deploys medieval history to authorize his own cross-temporal associations, he renders the witch as a particularly hybrid, irregular figure, and one with a specifically, if ambiguously, monstrous past. *Häxan* emerges, in this context, as a crucial index for an unruly intellectual history of enormous epistemological consequence. In this book, then, we are focused on unraveling the complexities of Christensen's *Häxan*, yet we also read his work as a crucial analytic for wider matters. The witch sits at the center of this project, and her image resonates with analyses of a certain kind of monstrosity in gendered and historical terms. Precisely as a mother/model for the later figure of the hysteric, the witch highlights a diverse asynchrony of gender, one keyed to the representational politics surrounding the female subject and her male examiners, whether persecutors or rescuers.

We will start, then, by suggesting that the witch, usually omitted from taxonomies of the "monster," might be read as a crucial subcategory of the monstrous in a time out-of-joint. The witch-as-monster signals both a category crisis and a

---

[4] The best modern edition of the text is *The Hammer of Witches: A Complete Translation of the Malleus Maleficarum*, ed. and trans. Christopher S. Mackay (Cambridge, UK: Cambridge University Press, 2009).

temporal paradox. And *Häxan*—with its crossing of "medieval" and "modern," its juxtaposition of documentation with historicized fantasy, its confused rendering of the witch as (alternately) victim to internal conflicts, and/or the member of a persecuted underclass—offers veritable "one stop shopping" for analyzing the temporal and libidinal categories important to this captivatingly perverse history. Christensen's film offers a fascinating opportunity to display the fissures and fault lines of the witch as a medieval monster in history, and our attention to the monstrous witch eventually pays off in a reading of the gender politics of *Häxan*'s monstrous medievalism.

⌒— 1: SEASONS OF THE WITCH

If popular magazines circa 2013 are any indication, the figure of the witch remains a "go-to" girl for Modern Horror. The popular cable series, *American Horror Story*, focused a recent season on a coven of witches, and the upcoming film adaptation of *Into the Woods* stars Meryl Streep, with gorgeously witchy visuals, in the main role. Gothic signifiers proliferate in these visual texts, usually to a distinctly medievalizing effect. We have seen such associations before. Nineteenth-century literature gave us the Gothic spaces of Victor Hugo's *The Hunchback of Notre Dame*.[5] By the early 20th century, and with the advent of film, a "medieval" iconography of horror seemed if not ubiquitous at least alive and well—the evil Rotwang from Fritz Lang's *Metropolis* (1927) is caught in a twilight world between gothic black magic and futuristic science as is, of course, Christensen's anachronistic meditation on the "medieval" history of witchcraft in *Häxan*.

In these and other contexts, the figure of the witch regularly crosses boundaries (temporal and narrative) or confuses categories (epistemological and cognitive). In this

---

[5] For a reading of Hugo's medievalism as important to the Gothic in subsequent decades, see Elizabeth Emery, *Romancing the Cathedral: Gothic Architecture in Fin-de-Siècle French Culture* (Albany: SUNY Press, 2001), especially 14–22.

regard, one might expect that the witch would figure prominently in the emerging field dedicated to elucidating the problems and pleasures of category confusion: Monster Studies. A cross-historical set of inquiries with an explicit interest in figures of the "in-between," Monster Studies engages what Asa S. Mittman calls "the oddities of creation," those "somewhat magical" figures occupying a place "outside of the ordinary."[6] Dedicated to wide-ranging inclusivity, Monster Studies generally welcomes scholars (and monsters) of an enormous historical, temporal, and geographic range. Yet the witch has been kept apart from its array of strange creatures. Publications in the field silently ignore her. She has seemed, perhaps, a monstrous creature too far, or, alternately, a creature not quite monstrous enough.

Such a problem of definition might instead offer the best case for her inclusion. The monster, as Jeffrey Jerome Cohen put it decades ago, "is harbinger of category crisis,"[7] and questions of definition regularly bedevil its categorical aspect. The field as a whole has made such crises constitutive, and crucial to the monster's cultural power. As Mittman does when, in the introduction to the *Ashgate Companion to Monster Studies*, he renders the power of the monster in active terms: the monster "defies the human power to subjugate through categorization."[8] Monsters are, for this very reason, "cognitively threatening,"[9] even "a

---

[6] Asa Simon Mittman, *Maps and Monsters in the Middle Ages* (New York: Routledge, 2006), 6.

[7] Jeffrey Jerome Cohen, "Monster Culture (Seven Theses)," in *Monster Theory: Reading Culture*, ed. Jeffrey Jerome Cohen (Minneapolis: University of Minnesota Press, 1996), 6 [3–25].

[8] Asa Simon Mittman, "Introduction: The Impact of Monsters and Monster Studies," in *The Ashgate Research Companion to Monsters and the Monstrous*, eds. Asa Simon Mittman and Peter Dendle (Farnham, UK: Ashgate, 2012), 7 [1–16].

[9] Mittman, "Introduction," 8 (quoting Noël Carroll, *The Philosophy of Horror.*)

revolution in the very logic of meaning."[10] So, too, is the figure of the witch. This is, in fact, precisely what makes her so interesting to Freud, to Weyer, to Christensen, and to a history of witch hunters, all of whom relentlessly, if unsuccessfully, try to define, to classify and sub-classify, to "solve" the problem of her testimony, or to pin her down.

Admittedly, on the score of the witch's ability to "defy" subjugation "through categorization," the historical record is mixed. If, as Cohen also once put it, the "monster always escapes,"[11] the same cannot be said for all those particular women accused of being, or of having been, witches themselves, many of whom were tortured or put to death. Historians of witchcraft are rightfully wary of reifying the "witch" as some kind of cross-cultural or essential reality; local studies deftly attend to the particular bodies and particular histories, the specific localities and specific seasons relevant to the "witch craze." As historical people, witches haunt across time; they are less monsters themselves than victims of monstrous treatment, denizens of the bad old days when inquisitors stalked the heretical and the heterodox, the renegade and the unlucky alike. Yet we would emphatically assert that while such historical people show the troubling effect of the witch as the monstrous, they are not identical to that figure. The witch's monstrosity is more diffuse, a figure and a body produced in cultural transactions across a range of times, places, figures, and disciplines. She represents, in this way, the monster as diffuse "cultural body."[12] When was she real and when was she not? Who can tell? "The binary of real and unreal,"

---

[10] Cohen, "Monster Culture," 7, citing Barbara Johnson, "Translator's Introduction," in Jacques Derrida, *Dissemination*, trans. Barbara Johnson (Chicago: University of Chicago Press, 1981), vii–xxxv.

[11] Cohen, "Monster Culture," 4.

[12] Cohen, "Monster Culture," 4.

writes Mittman, "is problematic when applied to monsters."[13]

The witch seems to us uncannily pertinent to all such claims. Undeniably human, she dangerously tarries with the extra-human;[14] she marks the confusion of fantasy with history, and blurs the borders of victim and victimizer, insides and outsides, pleasures and perversions. The problem of the real and unreal converges in the witch quite precisely. We will venture further: she not only crosses those boundaries, but also, and paradoxically, explicitly *contains* them, displaying real and unreal as a crucial internal problem. On all these grounds, the figure of the witch might well be Monster, Exhibit A. For what more compelling claim can be made for a figure in whom the real and unreal converge in impossible—and troubling— epistemological conflict?

Yet the problem of where to locate monstrosity within her complex history persists. For Heinrich Kramer and other inquisitors, witches themselves are clearly monstrous. But from the vantage of historical distance we can ask whether monstrosity figures in those suffering persecution for being witches or in those doing the persecuting. Precisely on account of such questions, precisely because of the shifts over time as to the answers given, and precisely because the witch stalks the boundary of fantasy and history, we will argue that her figure can shed considerable light on how monsters can confront historical change. We explore the witch as monster in order to track her altogether ambivalent historical timing, a temporality entwined with lurid pleasures as much as with remedy or punishment. Christensen's *Häxan* sheds light on these features of the witch, offering a view of her uncanny temporality, a "category crisis" rendered in cross-temporal terms. Or, to put it

---

[13] Mittman, "Introduction," 4.
[14] As Cohen puts it in the Preface to *Monster Theory*, "monster and human are coincipient" (xi).

another way, *häxan* (literally, the witch) "through the ages," becomes a figure for "progress" that, paradoxically, puts progress on notice. Persecuted by medieval torturers, probed by psychoanalysts, photographed by physicians or documentary filmmakers, the witch persists in the hysteric, repeating "through the ages," yet with a difference.

This last point marks one more reason why we wish to think the witch alongside the monstrous: her continuous existence over centuries also offers access to an interesting subcategory of medievalism. If, as Mittman also compellingly puts it, "the monster is known through its effect, its impact,"[15] then the witch (bedeviling to influential thinkers for centuries) seems emblematic of a certain kind of distributive monstrous effect. Unlike many of the other categories of monster (whose aspect and threat proliferate in particular times and spaces), the figure of the witch confuses repeatedly, at diverse historical moments, although in strangely familiar ways. This monstrous witch stops change—not dead, but living—in its tracks. A monster documented but not realized, photographed but never captured, the witch is named and renamed, but never named securely. Always threatening to reemerge in other times and places, in this aspect the witch "always escapes."[16]

Conventional accounts of the history of the discourse of monstrosity frequently (if not universally) describe the shift from premodern to modern times as a shift from the religious register to the scientific. What was once a portent of the divine becomes a specimen for medical classification; a creature of sin and disorder to be redeemed by God is recast as a victim of disease or pathology in need of diagnosis and cure. Rosemarie Thomson's account is emblematic: "The trajectory of historical change," she writes, "can be characterized simply as a movement from a narra-

---

[15] Mittman, "Introduction," 6.
[16] Cohen, "Monster Culture," 4.

tive of the marvelous to a narrative of the deviant. As modernity develops in Western culture . . . the prodigious
monster transforms into a pathological revelation. . . .
What was taken as a [religious] portent shifts to a site of
[scientific] progress. In brief, wonder becomes error."[17]
Attentive to the specificity of science, such histories offer
considerable explanatory power regarding early medical
classification of bodily deformity and "strange births."

Yet if, by the 19th century, non-fictional treatments of
"monstrous bodies" veered away from religious wonder
and toward medical classification, fictional accounts never
quite kept to that path. Even during the Age of Science,
monstrosity was not easily delimited to the scientific
realm. This is yet another verification of Bruno Latour's
insight: we have never been modern. The regulatory re-
gime of the monstrous can, in other words and as Michel
Foucault has long since taught us, be productive for all
manner of alternative orders and powers. [18]

---

[17] Rosemarie Garland Thomson, "Introduction: From Wonder
to Error—A Genealogy of Freak Discourse in Modernity," in
Freakery: Cultural Spectacles of the Extraordinary Body, ed. Rosemarie Garland Thomson (New York: New York University
Press, 1996), 3 [1–19]. Thomson's analysis highlights the material histories of the Freak Show in 19th-century America, and
the larger story she tells involves the process whereby U.S. capi-
talism undertook the standardizations of gender, race, sexuality,
and physical disability through display and proliferation of discourse of Freakery. Not coincidentally, the progression from
religious to scientific categories is also one primary story told
about the development of the category of "race" in the Middle
Ages.

[18] Michel Foucault, *Abnormal: Lectures at the College de France,
1974-1975*, eds. Valerio Marchetti and Antonella Salomini,
trans. Graham Burchell (New York: Picador, 2003). See also
Karma Lochrie, *Heterosyncrasies: Female Sexuality When Normal
Wasn't* (Minneapolis: University of Minnesota Press, 2003), especially Chapter 1, "Have We Ever Been Normal?" (1–25).

The conventional account, helpful as it is, cannot explain the witch as a modern figure staged as medieval; it overlooks the commonalities between the discourses of monstrosity during the two eras. For while it is true that medieval monstrosities were not described in the scientific registers popular in later times, they were certainly imagined as signs of error. However wondrous, medieval monsters frequently signified "error" as sin, deformity, or perversion, a fact that reminds us that "error" functions equally easily (though not identically) in the religious as in the scientific registers.[19] Thomson's own language suggests as much: even as scientific code, the monster beckons in religious terms, a site for "revelation." This also means that we should not necessarily assume that a religious apprehension of the marvelous ushered in a discourse of premodern monstrosity that was kinder or gentler than its modern analogue.[20] Indeed, both older texts and modern film share a fascination with monstrous embodiments precisely as a fascination with "perverse" error. Analyses of medieval representations of monstrosity suggest that such figures often stand in for the heterodox elements of culture, elements that might simultaneously purvey and work to dis-

---

[19] For a review of relevant material see Bettina Bildhauer and Robert Mills, eds., *The Monstrous Middle Ages* (Cardiff: University of Wales Press, 2003).

[20] See Caroline Walker Bynum, "Wonder," *American Historical Review* 102.1 (Feb. 1997): 1–17, and Stephen Greenblatt, *Marvelous Possessions: The Wonder of the New World* (Chicago: University of Chicago Press, 1991). Here we depart from treatments of medieval "marveling" by Bynum and Greenblatt which each emphasize medieval magnanimity about foreignness in contrast to later times. Space prevents a more patient explication of this disagreement, but one can be found in Patricia Clare Ingham, "In Contrayez Straunge: Colonial Relations, British Identity, and *Sir Gawain and the Green Knight*," *New Medieval Literatures* 4 (2001): 61–94.

lodge hegemonic institutions and ideologies. Such work has opened important questions regarding, for instance, ideologies of masculinity in the Middle Ages and/or how a deft use of psychoanalysis might help us to understand medieval culture in all its historicity.

Not all medievalists, however, have welcomed these developments. Some, like historians Gabrielle Spiegel and Paul Freedman, have argued that drawing attention to representations of monsters in medieval texts misrepresents the period, returning us to a very old and conservative view of the Middle Ages, and naturalizing the identification of the medieval as stereotypically history's grotesque.[21] Spiegel and Freedman remind us that in the early decades of the twentieth century, historians like Charles Homer Haskins and Joseph Strayer argued vociferously that the period be viewed as a time of rationality and intellectual rigor, a formative era during which a variety of social, cultural, and political institutions originated. In the wake of this effort, the current interest in medieval monsters, Spiegel and Freedman argue, merely plays into the hands of those who have not learned the lessons that Haskins and Strayer taught us, those who wish to see the period as nothing but backward. It is thus their opinion that current work on medieval monsters puts at risk the massive accomplishment of an entire generation of medievalists. While we disagree with the scare tactics implicit in this essay, Spiegel and Freedman nonetheless make a cru-

---

[21] Paul Freedman and Gabrielle Spiegel, "Medievalisms Old and New: the Rediscovery of Alterity in North American Medieval Studies," *American Historical Review* 103.3 (1998): 577–704. For responses, see Paul Strohm, *Theory and the Premodern Text* (Minneapolis: University of Minnesota Press, 2000), 149–162, and Patricia Clare Ingham, "Contrapuntal Histories," in *Postcolonial Moves: Medieval Through Modern*, eds. Patricia Clare Ingham and Michelle R. Warren (New York: Palgrave Macmillan, 2003), 47–70.

cial historiographic point. We must consider a larger and longer comparative history, one that analyzes later associations between the medieval and the "monstrous."

One such convergence dates to the early decades of the twentieth century, the time when Christensen's work first appeared. This era witnessed a proliferation of discourses of monstrosity linked both to historical and (if differently) to religious controversy. It was then, for instance, that Haskins and fellow historian Charles Lea argued for a reconsideration of the rational insights of the High Middle Ages, suggesting that the germ of modern civil arrangements could be traced back to the twelfth century, yet it was also then that Pope Pius X insisted upon a return to traditional scholastic method, condemning certain Catholic philosophers' fascination with secular "Modernism" as a habit "disfigured by perverse doctrines and monstrous errors";[22] it was then that *Malleus Maleficarum*, Heinrich Kramer's infamous 1486 handbook for hunting witches, was first translated into English by Montague Summers, who would characterize that translation and publication of *Malleus* as particularly pertinent to the ills of the modernist century, a "world of confusion, of Bolshevism, of anarchy and licentiousness" (1928);[23] it was then, finally, that

---

[22] "Pascendi Dominic Gregis," Encyclical of Pope Pius X on the Doctrines of the Modernists (1907), http://www.vatican.va/holy _father/pius_x/encyclicals/documents/hf_p-x_enc_19070908_ pascendi-dominici-gregis_en.html.

[23] This citation is taken from the "Introduction" to Montague Summers' 1928 English edition of the famous handbook of witches, for decades the only available English edition: Heinrich Kramer and James Sprenger, *Malleus Maleficarum* (1486), ed. and trans. Montague Summers (rpt. London: Dover Publications, 1971), xl. Summers' personal history is strange and untangling it is not easy. An ordained priest and later bishop in the Old Catholic Church of the Utrecht Succession, he was a prolific writer and quirky figure around London in the early 20th cen-

Christensen's *Häxan* juxtaposed the religious excesses of medieval witches and witch hunters with the modern doctor of psychology and the hysteric.

In both its "medieval" and "modern" incarnations, the witch points to vexing epistemological issues for the cultures of which it is a part. What does it mean, we ask, that these two eras share an interest in the epistemological question of how to disentangle fantasy from "the real," and a concern with authorities and their oppressions? What does it mean that these questions are focused so persistently on women? These questions will illuminate the incoherence of Christensen's film, itself a vehicle for purveying the association of the medieval with the monstrous still with us today. On the one hand, the retrospective diagnosis of the witch-as-hysteric that Christensen cites seems to register the standard view of monstrous development just described: from religious wonder to scientific classification. We will argue, instead, that Christensen's film shows that the figure of the "witch" returns as the "hysteric" not so as to track "progress" from religious superstition to scientific rationality, but precisely as a figure for category crisis, for unsolvable epistemological problems.

To unravel the medievalism of Christensen's film, we must first turn to select early modern texts and recent scholarship concerning European witchcraft. We begin with the historical specificity of witchcraft, as the question emerged in Europe in early modernity, paying special attention to debates over the meaning of witchcraft testimony, as evinced in the different positions taken by Kramer, author of *Malleus Maleficarum* (1486) and Johann Weyer, author of *De praestigiis daemonum* (1563). Kramer and Weyer, as we shall see, represent two distinct early modern positions on *maleficia*, and they disagree as to whether women's testimony of their dalliance with the devil ought to be given credence as real or dismissed as fantastical im-

---

tury. A history of Summers himself still waits to be written.

aginings. Christensen's film recapitulates features of this debate even as it relocates it to the early twentieth century. His witch, in a time out-of-joint, follows a track set in multiple centuries: the fifteenth, the sixteenth, the nineteenth and twentieth. Such untimely temporality takes a monstrous medieval aspect.

✐— 2: *MALEFICIA* AND BELIEF

In a letter dated January 17, 1897, addressed to William Fleiss, Sigmund Freud suggests a medieval genealogy for his (eventually controversial) studies of hysteria [*hysterie-Urgeschichte*]:

> What would you say, by the way, if I told you that all of my brand-new prehistory of hysteria is already known and was published a hundred times over, though several centuries ago? Do you remember that I always said that the medieval theory of possession held by the ecclesiastical courts was identical with our theory of a foreign body and the splitting of consciousness? But why did the devil who took possession of the poor things invariably abuse them sexually and in a loathsome manner? Why are their confessions under torture so like the communications made by my patients in psychic treatment? Sometime soon I must delve into the literature on this subject.[24]

---

[24] Jeffrey Mouissaieff Masson, ed. and trans., *The Complete Letters of Sigmund Freud to Wilhelm Fliess, 1887-1904* (Cambridge, MA: Belknap Press, 1985), 224.

The literature to which Freud alludes is the infamous 15th-century manual for witch hunters, *Malleus Maleficarum*. By the very next week, Freud would attest more explicitly to his interest in it.

Acclaimed by some as the most influential European handbook for early modern witch hunters, the *Malleus Maleficarum* (1486) to which Freud obliquely refers in his letter to Fleiss, is itself controversial as a source for information on European witch trials of the early modern period. But before considering Christensen's immediate context—a context that included the influence of the *Malleus* on the history of psychoanalysis and psychiatry—we need to attend to the complexities of Kramer's own monstrous figures. The importance and influence of this lurid handbook for recognizing, interrogating, and punishing witches has yet to be settled. Select local studies from the period offer little evidence of the juridical use of the infamous manual, leading some historians to insist that its influence in the implementation of the inquisition has been much exaggerated. What we know of the publishing history, however, would seem to suggest the opposite. Sydney Anglo, for example, points out that the *Malleus* "was reissued more frequently than any other major witch-hunting manual; it was long the most commonly cited; and it remained one of the works which the opponents of persecution sought especially to refute."[25] Nor is this the only source of textual controversy. The manual's authorship has also been the subject of debate, with some arguing that Jacob

---

[25] Sydney Anglo, "Evident Authority and Authoritative Evidence: The *Malleus maleficarum*," in *The Damned Art: Essays in the Literature of Witchcraft*, ed. Sydney Anglo (London: Routledge, 1977), 4 [1–31]. On the debate among historians, see Kathleen Biddick, *The Shock of Medievalism* (Durham: Duke University Press, 1998), especially "The Devil's Anal Eye: Inquisitorial Optics and Ethnographic Authority," 105–134, and 237–239: n15.

Sprenger's supposed endorsement of the project is a for-
gery devised by Kramer to encourage the approval of the
faculty of Theology at the University of Cologne—support
necessary for the publication of the manuscript.[26]

The indeterminate nature of the book's history is fitting
since epistemological issues are central to the witch craze
itself. Histories of witchcraft in medieval and early modern
Europe seek to undermine such trans-historical associations in favor of the specificity and diversity of Europe's
particular cases; yet such studies, as we shall see, also regularly suggest the ways that the female witch converges on
mixed or hybrid categories, and on the seam joining insides to outsides. Even within the confines of Europe,
practice varied as to both time and place. In the premodern period, worries over *maleficia* emerged within a broad-
er discourse about the discernment of spirits, a concern
engaged equally on the sides of saints or sinners. Premodern hagiography persistently questioned the influence of
spirits as a problem of interpretation, emphasizing the dif-
ficulty in discerning the true nature of visions. Claims of
divine visitation were notoriously slippery: not only might
such claims be false, but visions themselves could result
from the promptings of evil spirits masquerading as good.
In the medieval tradition, such issues engaged insides and
outsides. How might we assess the nature and effect of
external forces on interior holiness? As Nancy Caciola puts
it, "medieval discussions of how to discern spirits always
pulse back and forth between the two poles of interior and

---

[26] On this point see Walter Stephens, "Witches Who Steal Penises: Impotence and Illusion in *Malleus Maleficarum*," *Journal of
Medieval and Early Modern Studies* 28.3 (1998): 495–529. For an
alternative reading of the clerical position, see also Michael D.
Bailey, "From Sorcery to Witchcraft: Clerical Conceptions of
Magic in the Later Middle Ages," *Speculum* 74.4 (2001): 960–
990.

exterior."[27] Such concerns will continue in Catholic hagiographic writings into the early modern period (as, for instance, in the works of Teresa of Avila or John of the Cross). The saint or mystic might be said, in this larger context, to serve as an historical Doppelgänger to the witch.

Early Modern debates over *maleficia* took up some of the problems of spiritual discernment in the context of doctrinal difference and reformist critique. Yet early modern belief in *maleficia* also inherited features of earlier debates about popular or folk religious practice. During the Middle Ages, questions of supernaturalism proceeded from metaphysical views (inherited from Aristotle) concerning the power of invisible spirits in the basic working of the universe. Scholastic writers offered a variety of responses to such questions, particularly insofar as they converged on pastoral questions related to popular religious practice. While it was not the case, so Euan Cameron argues, that "the medieval Church was complacent about popular belief," the scholastic authorities disagreed widely as to specifics "beyond the obvious and usually quite unhelpful fact that the vast majority of clergy vehemently disapproved of . . . demonic magic."[28] In his informative history of European supernaturalism in the Middle Ages and Renaissance, Cameron documents the various ways that scholastic metaphysics came, gradually, to oppose traditional folk beliefs. The Early Modern period, he stresses, witnessed a gradual tightening of focus about these matters as such disagreements became opportunities for religious polemic and reformist critique.

---

[27] Nancy Caciola, *Discerning Spirits: Divine and Demonic Possession in the Middle Ages* (Ithaca: Cornell University Press, 2003), 20.

[28] Euan Cameron, *Enchanted Europe: Superstition, Reason, and Religion, 1250-1750* (New York: Oxford University Press, 2011), 139.

The result was a pitched polemical debate aimed at doctrinal matters but tracking a circuit of claims about demonic influence. Enter Kramer's *Malleus*. Designed in tripartite form, the *Malleus* provides, in part one, a series of authorities in support of the existence of the devil and witchcraft; in part two, an encyclopedia of witchcraft methods and ways to combat the same; and, in part three, confessional and interrogatory techniques (including torture) designed to produce self-incriminating testimony as verification of a truth otherwise improvable. Inquisitors like the Dominican Kramer were concerned to prove as "fact" the stories that witches had engaged in sexual congress and marriages with actual devils.[29] Testimonies from

---

[29] On this point see Stephens, "Witches Who Steal Penises." Stephens describes the Witch hunts as "a war on reality that produced a massacre of women" (517), making clear the epistemological anxieties for religion as a root cause; yet his unwillingness to consider the epistemological problem raised by fantasy leads to some blindness in his analysis. The following is exemplary: "Whatever Kramer says, his real purpose for torturing the woman into [her] confession, (assuming the story is not pure mythomania) was to reassure himself that the Eucharist could do something other than just lie there like any other lump of bread. His rhetoric of crime and outrage runs counter to a logic of sacramentality and hope" (514). Here Stephens's parenthetical remark itself raises the very issues that preoccupied Freud and that seem to beg for more nuanced psychoanalytic attention. Furthermore, this has consequences for his reading of the meaning of the clerical choice of the female victim: "Witchcraft theorists were misogynists, but the witch-hunt was not a war on women; it was a *war on reality* that produced a massacre of women, along with a sizable massacre of men and children. . . . the fundamental anxiety of witchcraft theory had never been the impotence of men or the power of women, but the possibility that God himself might be impotent, indifferent, or illusory" (517). Reading this in a larger history of epistemology and gender (like that which we attempt in this chapbook) can make legible the logic of links between a "war on women" with "a war on reality." Chal-

the women themselves were not, he would write, "phantasies" or "fancies." The circular logic of the *Malleus* has been noted many times before: testimony could be falsified; protestations of innocence were likely read as signs of guilt. [30]

Kramer hunted witches not, so Walter Stephens argues, because he was a "true believer but rather because he was incapable of belief."[31] Stephens reads the Inquisitor's project as the result of a profound anxiety surrounding doctrinal controversies at the time of the Reformation. Kramer's response to such doubts resulted in a text marked less by irrationality than by a "hyperactivity" of reason: Kramer's argument is, as Stephens puts it, "an extreme refinement of rationality and logic"; and "Kramer's monsters," he opines, "are not produced by the sleep or dreaming of reason, . . . but rather by its insomnia and hyperactivity."[32] The *Malleus* was, in this way, an extension of high scholasticism, "one of the last and most oblique strategies that Catholicism, and scholasticism in particular, attempted for explaining away [the] dissonance" between empiricism and sacramental efficacy.[33] Stephens makes Kramer's logic

---

lenges to the omnipotence of God portend challenges to the power of the male knower, particularly with regard to female interiors.

[30] Some, like Anglo, contrast the uses of authority and evidence here to a later scientific method. "What constituted a conclusive argument in the period between the fifteenth and late seventeenth centuries? . . . It was something very different from what scholars now regard as a valid argument: that is the deliberate attempt at objectivity; inductive reasoning; the evaluation of evidence rather than its mere accumulation; conscious skepticism of received authorities; and above all else, the process of constantly testing hypotheses by controlled experiment" (Anglo, "Evident Authority and Authoritative Evidence," 3).

[31] Stephens, "Witches Who Steal Penises," 497.

[32] Stephens, "Witches Who Steal Penises," 505–506.

[33] Stephens, "Witches Who Steal Penises," 499.

clear: "The inquisitorial mind fears nothing more than an autonomous human imagination, for if devils do not control the vagaries of imagination, then they may actually be vagaries of the imagination."[34] Unfettered imagination, that is, may be even more worrisome than demonic influence.

Yet the possibility that the supposed witches were victims of fantasy or delusion will persist in response to Kramer's work, constituting one of the main critiques leveled against his text. Those critical of the Catholic inquisitors argued that the devil himself prompted the gullibility of Catholic priests, influencing inquisitors to believe testimony that could not possibly be true. According to men like Jacob Weyer—author of the first, though arguably the most flawed, attempt at a systematic refutation of the *Malleus*—the victim's confessions of unnatural things could just as equally offer proof of delusion, or be motivated by ill will, confusion, duress, or illness rather more than demonic visitation. Regarding the possibility of false testimony by the accused, he writes:

> We must ascertain whether the troubles and calamities which the [Witches] claim to have brought upon others are really such or whether they are caused naturally. And if it is discovered that some persons have been injured or that they have suffered disease or loss of property in such a way that the ills now seem to have been brought about by these other parties who have confessed to them, there must be a thorough investigation to find by what means, materials, or instruments the crimes have been perpetrated, and to decide whether those means, materials, or instruments are suitable for producing such effects. . . . Just as one cannot rely upon the confes-

---

[34] Stephens, "Witches Who Steal Penises," 507.

sion of a melancholic person or a mentally incompetent person, so, too, punishment should not rashly be inflicted on the basis of a confession by these women, unless from the known circumstances, and from clear demonstration. . . . The proofs must be clearer than the noonday sun, especially in the so-called criminal action—this is the commendable view of the legal experts—because in this matter of *maleficium* many things are said confusedly (as a result of ill will), or under the stress of disease or the loss of property. The statements betray a lack of faith, because the persons who make them do not entrust themselves wholeheartedly to God's just wishes.[35]

In contrast to Kramer's emphasis upon the confusion caused *by* witches ("they could bring the whole world to utter confusion"),[36] Weyer reads the testimony against witches as *itself* confused, likely originating in a wide range of causes, including relatively common human frailties or aggressions, the product of a variety of "stresses," whether internal (disease) or external (loss of property). Weyer distinguishes *maleficia* from the host of things with which it might be confused: ill will, disease, stress, all here distinct from demonic possession, yet all equally betray "a lack of faith." Yet in a move that will later prove important for the history of psychiatry, Weyer also explicitly links accused witches to the "melancholic . . . or mentally incompetent

---

[35] *Witches, Devils, and Doctors in the Renaissance: Johann Weyer, De Praestigiis Daemonum*, ed. George Mora, trans. John Shea, Medieval and Renaissance Texts and Studies (Binghamton, NY: MRTS, 1991), Book 6, Chapter 10.

[36] "quia sic perimere possent totum mundum": Kramer, question 1 (1). Quotations from the *Malleus* are taken from Mackay's 2009 Cambridge edition, *The Hammer of Witches* (see full citation in note 4).

person," arguing that it is their accusers, not the witches themselves, who are guilty of confusion and a "lack of faith."

Considered as a response to the *Malleus*, Weyer's *Demonum* stakes a claim on the theological question of how devils work in the world. And just as Stephens reads a "hyperactivity of logic" in Kramer's anxious work, Christopher Baxter emphasizes Weyer's writings as religious polemic, a "curious mixture of tolerance and intolerance, perceptiveness and credulity."[37] Baxter emphasizes the paradoxical nature of Weyer's own achievement: more important than Weyer "the humanitarian physician, concerned with the objective nature of melancholia" is Weyer "the Lutheran practitioner, incensed by Catholic idolatry."[38] This had a significant downside. "Weyer's disastrous mistake," Baxter later asserts, "is to discuss magic and witchcraft in the context of religious polemic. Conversely, his most significant achievement is perhaps his incautious discussion of religion in terms of magic and witchcraft: Christianity and diabolic magic are comparable, complementary forces."[39]

Taken together, Kramer and Weyer track the early modern theological debate on *maleficia* occurring on the conti-

---

[37] Christopher Baxter, "Unsystematic Psychopathology," in *The Damned Art*, ed. Anglo, 63 [53–75].

[38] Baxter, "Unsystematic Psychopathology," 61–62. Weyer's project distinguishes weak women used *by* the devil from superstitious male magicians (a category that implicitly includes Catholic priests, the main targets of Weyer's attack) who actively, and more nefariously, *use* the devil. Baxter argues that Weyer failed "by evoking the counterblast of two intellectually outstanding writers, not just his fellow Lutheran Erastus, but also Jean Bodin, a man who had just acquired a European reputation for his political masterpiece, the *Republique*. Indeed, Bodin's *Demonomanie* largely adopts Weyer's theory of magic" (71).

[39] Baxter, "Unsystematic Psychopathology," 71.

nent. It is important to remember at this point that far from constituting a debate between "rational science" and "superstitious religiosity," the various positions on *maleficia* are largely theological in nature (with the *Malleus* closely identified with Roman Catholicism, and Weyer's work with Lutheranism). Weyer's critique emphasizes Kramer's "superstition" in a polemic leveled not against religion as such, but against the sacramental theology (and clerical features) of Roman Catholicism. And even as a "defense of witches," Weyer's project "badly misfired," "evoking the counterblast of intellectually outstanding writers" (including Jean Bodin) ready to refute it.[40] The debate would continue for some time.

Weyer's critique of the *Malleus*—both his polemics and his link of Catholicism with superstition and magic—will cast a very long shadow outside of any doctrinal register. The contrast between Weyer and Kramer's accounts of witchcraft would become, for some, the prehistory of the contrast between modern secular science and medieval religious superstition. Medical historian Gregory Zilboorg, for example, will cast Weyer as "father" to the modern psychiatric profession. In a series of important lectures given at Johns Hopkins in 1935, Zilboorg praises Weyer's "scientific skepticism" as a sign of Renaissance renewal and the advent of humanism, judging Weyer to inaugurate the rationalist "factual" approach productive for the science of psychology: "Through a factual approach Weyer seeks not only to undermine the authority of the devil but to prepare a sufficient foundation for a rational physiological psy-

---

[40] Baxter, "Unsystematic Psychopathology," 71. Baxter concludes that Weyer's most "disastrous mistake," is nonetheless linked to his "most significant achievement": while "discuss[ing] magic and witchcraft in the context of religious polemic" makes his text liable for easy refutation, "his incautious discussion of religion in terms of magic and witchcraft" also meant that "Christianity and diabolic magic emerge as comparable, complementary forces."

chology and psychopathology."[41] On the one hand, it is this aspect of Weyer's work that grounds its importance to Jean-Martin Charcot and his students, researchers on hysteria at the Hospital of Salpêtrière in late nineteenth-century Paris. Freud was a student of Charcot's and this may well account for his decision to include Weyer's treatise among his 1906 list of the 10 "most significant" books ever written. On the other hand, to see the triumph of "modern science" over "medieval religion" in this history requires a determined refusal to acknowledge either the "hyperactivity of reason" in Kramer's work, or doctrinal polemic in Weyer's.

The epistemological consequences of the debate between Kramer and Weyer will be important to Charcot and to Freud, and the role of gender is crucial in each case: at issue is whether women's testimony of their dalliance with the devil ought to be given credence as real or imagined. Yet even this history does not proceed in a straight line for, as we shall see, Freud's interest in Weyer will also be read as keyed to a "superstition" rendered "medieval." The tendentious opposition between religious superstition and scientific knowledge will feature prominently in various historical narratives on the topic, including the one that drives Christensen's *Häxan*. Indeed, this influential association explains in part that film's fixation on witchcraft as an insistently medieval phenomenon, a fixation that seems especially strange considering the extensive historical bibliography that Christensen apparently consulted. The "medieval" emerges, in the light of this paradox, as a category deployed for something other than historical accuracy. Yet before turning to Christensen's film, we still need to probe the epistemological problems raised by the testi-

---

[41] Gregory Zilboorg, "The Medical Man and the Witch Towards the Close of the Sixteenth Century," *Bulletin of the New York Academy of Medicine* 11.10 (1935): 579–607.

mony of the witch. These are the problems that Freud engaged; and these are the problems that Christensen's medievalism attempts, though not entirely successfully, to put to rest.

ᐱ— 3: TESTIMONY TROUBLES

At its base, witchcraft, whether as espoused by Dominican Inquisitors or Lutheran physicians, channeled theological debates shot through with epistemological problems. It was not, as we have seen, a war between irrational "superstition" and rational "science": religious polemic produced Weyer's putatively "rational" treatise, and scholastic hyper-rationality runs through Kramer's "religious" one. A host of questions were at issue, including the nature of evidence; the discernment of spirits; knowledge of the subject's interior; the trustworthiness of what can be seen; the reliability or efficacy of folk traditions; whether and how dictums of faith can reconcile physical facts; the methods by which inquisitors acquired and verified their knowledge of demonic activities, and the production of knowledge about sex and sexuality.[42] Both Weyer's and

---

[42] Some, like Anglo, contrast the uses of authority and evidence here to a later scientific method: "What constituted a conclusive argument in the period between the fifteenth and late seventeenth centuries? . . . It was something very different from what scholars now regard as valid argument: that is the deliberate attempt at objectivity; inductive reasoning; the evaluation of evidence rather than its mere accumulation; conscious scepticism of received authorities; and above all else, the process of constantly

Kramer's texts endeavor (if in different ways) to cope with crucial problems of knowledge, and with the disjunction between structures of belief and contradictory physical evidence.

Women's testimony proves particularly crucial for these thinkers. Kramer's "monsters," as Stephens calls them, were women; and Weyer protests that it is women who, whether filled with "ill will" or suffering from melancholia, are punished too "rashly on the basis of a confession." If the early modern problem of the witch developed out of a longstanding tradition concerning the discernment of spirits, it is striking the degree to which, by the early modern period, the interiors at issue (sexual as well as spiritual) came to be female. Stephens argues that the verifiability of women's testimony is a primary concern because of a crucial case important to the *Malleus*: the threat that the fact of impotence posed to confidence in God's control of human procreation. In Part I, Question 8, the Inquisitor considers "Whether sorceresses can impede the faculty to procreate (the sexual act)."[43] Answering in the affirmative, Kramer carefully outlines the circumstances under which "countless effects of sorcery can happen truly and really with God's permission."[44] Asserting the omnipotence of God is crucial to this work. If impotence were simply the result of the work of Satan, in defiance of God's command to procreate, Satan would be more powerful than God. But such a case was, for Kramer, impossible. Searching for circumstances under which God would permit such a thing to happen, Kramer persistently twins the sorceress's disordered spiritual interior with her sexual proclivities: a wife may be seeking other lovers; women wish to "create an opportunity to commit adultery." In these tendencies

---

testing hypotheses by controlled experiment" (Anglo, "Evident Authority and Authoritative Evidence," 3).

[43] Mackay, *The Hammer of Witches*, 187.

[44] Mackay, *The Hammer of Witches*, 188.

toward sin, "God gives more permission to the demons to act savagely against sinners than against the just."[45]

Asserting the power of demons emerges, in this context, as the evil twin to a belief in God's transformative power in the world. This makes clear, as Stephens points out, that so far as Kramer's text was concerned, "the impotence of men or the power of women" was not "the fundamental anxiety of witchcraft theory." Kramer was driven by "the possibility that God himself might be impotent, indifferent, or illusory."[46] The testimony of women to the reality of demonic influence served as the proof, paradoxically enough, for belief in God's power. In Kramer's "hyper-rational" logic, such testimony simply had to be true. The witch-hunts were, in this way, "a war on reality" that produced "a massacre of women."[47]

The question of whether the testimony of women counts as reliable evidence will, of course, also be crucial to that later infamous controversy, one that arguably still haunts the fields of psychiatry and psychoanalysis: that is, Freud's infamous revision of his seduction theory in favor of his theory of infantile sexuality. This revision would be famously criticized by Jeffrey Mousaieff Masson and others as a failure of Freudian science. As is well known, Freud revised earlier claims validating his patients' recollections as actual experiences of childhood sexual abuse at the hands of family members and friends; he argued, in the end, that many such memories, released in analysis, were the result of repressed guilt to do with the sexual fantasies of the children themselves. Critics, like Peter Swales, will adduce Freud's admiration for Weyer to intellectual timidity, unscientific error, and superstition. Emphasizing Freud's admiration of Weyer as crucial to the controversial

---

[45] Mackay, *The Hammer of Witches*, 189.
[46] Stephens, "Witches Who Steal Penises," 517.
[47] Stephens, "Witches Who Steal Penises," 505–506.

rethinking of his seduction theory, Swales argues that Freud's retreat from his earlier theory emerges not (as was claimed) from a rethinking based upon clinical data, but as a function of Freud's unacknowledged indebtedness to Weyer. For Swales, Freud's interest in Weyer figures his interest in all things medieval and, precisely as such, tracks a monstrous history whereby Freud crucially turned away from fact and toward error. Swales thus opposes Freud's interest in "medieval" witchcraft (and, not coincidentally, his interest in religion) to his work as a scientist.[48] As an episode in the history of the field of psychoanalysis, Swales argues, Freud's submerged medievalism compromises both a commitment to truth and his claims as a scientist.

Writing forty years before Swales, Zilboorg, we recall, would praise Weyer as the "father of psychiatry." Weyer's reading of female confession as a result of internal conflicts "undermine[s] the authority of the devil," Zilboorg argued, through "a factual approach," the latter attesting to the Lutheran physician's scientific *bonafides*.[49] Swales reads Weyer's influence (now, specifically on Freud) in opposite terms. The contrast between the positions taken by Zilboorg and by Swales strangely repeats the earlier debate between Weyer and Kramer but, and paradoxically, in reverse. In the earlier centuries, confidence in the truth of confession and in the real existence of the devil was critiqued in an alternative account in which confession was understood as engaged with a host of human desires, aggressions, and frailties. Yet by the last third of the twentieth century these positions emerge, only now reversed. In the 1970s, a view of confession as engaged with a host of desires and human frailties will be contested by the reality principle of not the devil but of sexual abusers (a devil in a

---

[48] Peter J. Swales, "A Fascination with Witches: Medieval Tales of Torture Altered the Course of Psychoanalysis," *The Sciences* 22.8 (1982): 21–25. Note the medievalism of Swales's lurid title.
[49] Zilboorg, "The Medical Man and the Witch," 579.

modern cast). Testimony to the existence of sexual abuse must be believed as true; and reports no matter how outlandish will be taken seriously and, in the United States, prosecuted to the full extent of the law. In the light of the history of the witch, it may not be only coincidental that allegations of widespread and rampant sexual abuses of children in childcare centers and preschools, such as the famous case of the McMartin Preschool in Manhattan Beach, California, included allegations of Satanic worship, cults, and rituals. Such a recurrence points to the persistence of this monstrous epistemological problem, the witch as harbinger of category crisis.

In a psychoanalytically-informed reading that interrogates crucial features of the problem of knowledge in the history of witchcraft, Kathleen Biddick suggests that the *Malleus Maleficarum* occupies a key role in the development of those epistemological methods important to the later knowledge/power systems reliant on eyewitness testimony, ethnography and history in particular. For Biddick, the figure of the devil provided Inquisitors and historians since with "a powerful optical device," such that accused women were subjected to an early ethnographic method, committed to making diabolic practice visible and thus evidentiary. This technique becomes foundational to the technologies of knowing that come down to us in the form of expert testimony and verifiable evidence:

> The devil serves as a kind of optical device that makes the inquisitor's [work] visible and therefore something that can be *counted as evidence*. The textual materialization of the devil that the *Malleus* sediments with such care enables the inquisitor to gaze at and see, make legible, an invisible world of the ethnos he is conjuring . . . . The devil offers a special kind of insight, what ethnographers today

would call a theoretical abstraction that promises the ethnographer "to get to the heart" of a culture.[50]

Witchcraft provided, in the face of intellectual uncertainty, a set of procedures for the verification of knowledge as evidence (juridical, but also empirical). If Weyer came, as Zilboorg argues, to inspire the field of psychiatry, Biddick's work reads Kramer's methods as equally crucial to later empirical procedures associated with disciplines in the social sciences. Inquisitorial technologies, she argues, remain sedimented in standard historicist and ethnographic methods regularized in later centuries. Biddick's work foregrounds the political and epistemological stakes in all such matters of testimony evidence. Biddick notes Freud's interest in the *Malleus* in passing: "even Sigmund Freud could not bear to part with his German translation as he stood before his bookshelves in Nazi Vienna making decisions about which books to leave behind and which to take along on his flight to London."[51]

---

[50] Biddick, *The Shock of Medievalism*, 116–117, emphasis in original.

[51] Biddick, *The Shock of Medievalism*, 108–109. These responses, just like the controversy itself, mark the line that joins imagination and fantasy (on the one hand), with truth, history, or fact (on the other). On this same boundary, edge, border, or seam, medievalism and the Middle Ages converge; over such terrain these two fields have been both joined and separated. Scholars pursuing those relations, such as John Ganim, Kathleen Biddick, or Thomas A. Prendergast and Stephanie Trigg, have emphasized the politics and passionate attachments spanning that edge. See John Ganim, *Medievalism and Orientalism: Three Essays on Literature, Architecture, and Cultural Identity* (New York: Palgrave, 2005), and Thomas Prendergast and Stephanie Trigg, *Medievalism and Its Discontents* (forthcoming). And in a spirit not unlike our own, Prendergast and Trigg have recently remarked on Freud's interest in medieval testimony about witches, considered as a "stumbling block" of consequence, an implicit

Memories of sexual abuse have raised problems for evidentiary juridical standards—problems associated most recently with "recovered memory syndrome"; this suggests instead a complicated position regarding the interpretation of testimony, and the evidence of remembered experience. It hints, too, at the degree to which Freud's point is larger, and more incisive than Swales admits, in large measure because Freud's medievalism is fairly nuanced: Freud turns to the medieval so as to ponder epistemological question about inquisitorial technologies, and thus about the reports he hears from his analysands. Yet, when Freud remarks on the analogies he saw between "his patients under psychic treatment" and witchcraft victims who "confessed under torture," he appropriates certain facets of Early Modern debates over witchcraft for this crucial question. Freud is struck by historical repetitions, by similarities between his clinical experience and the historical record. As he asks Fleiss: "Why did the devil who took possession of the poor things invariably abuse them sexually and in a loathsome manner? Why are their confessions under torture so like the communications made by my patients in psychic treatment?" These two questions concern the nature of confession as evidence, something that Weyer—as part of his critique of Catholic priests—explicitly calls into question.

Throughout her reading of the technologies of knowledge produced by the witch craze, Biddick reminds us of the important question of when and how testimony counts as real, a question crucial to both Freud's qualification of his seduction theory and to those critical of that qualification. Weyer's "science" did not, that is, repudiate religious superstition, as Zilboorg would have it. Instead, questions of verifiable evidence were split between "scientific" and

reminder that the discernment of "truth" regularly converges on fantasies of "punishment, and pleasure."

"ethnographic" methods. Problems of verification, and of truth, remain. And it is, thus, not at all coincidental that when the witch becomes refigured as the "hysteric," questions of testimony and fantasy will again reemerge. For the problem of testimony was not, it turns out, overcome with the "inquisitorial techniques" of the early moderns.

Freud's interest in the witches—his disdain for "medieval" inquisitors and his interest in Weyer's critique of them—does not revel in superstition so much as promote a reconsideration of the epistemological status of experience, memory, confession, or personal testimony as evidence. Yet insofar as he distrusted the inquisitors and the testimony thereby produced, insofar as the so-called "medieval" history of witchcraft displayed for him confession as a mode not of evidentiary truth, but of fantasy, Freud's "medievalism" provided him (perhaps paradoxically) with a skepticism powerful enough to challenge even the modern man of science. This is not, as Swales might have it, a turn to a medieval religious superstition, but rather a return to uncertainty about the nature of testimony, an epistemological crises long associated with the history of High Modernism.[52] Freud's medievalism shows this to be a

---

[52] Controversies over the epistemological consequences of psychoanalysis continue to obtain. Freud's thoughts on the knowledge produced by fantasy can be found in "New Introductory Lectures on Psycho-Analysis" (1933), *The Standard Edition of the Psychological Works of Sigmund Freud* [SE], ed. and trans. James A. Strachey, Vol. 22 (London: Hogarth Press, 1964), 1–182. In his analysis of the Freud's Schreiber case, Lacan develops the notion that the subject's knowledge is fundamentally paranoiac and, while distinct from psychosis, not entirely unrelated to it. See Jacques Lacan, "On a Question Preliminary to Any Possible Treatment of Psychosis," in *Ecrits: A Selection*, trans. Alan Sheridan (New York: W.W. Norton, 1977), 179–225. Psychoanalytic epistemologies press upon the gaps, contradictions, and distortions of our mechanisms of observation, language, and reason, and are thus engaged in revealing what the

modern, secular epistemological crisis that retroactively resonates with a medieval, religious past.

Like Freud, Christensen's 1922 film considers certain women of the Middle Ages alongside certain women of the 1920s, and all under the sign of the "witch." The final filmic chapter of *Häxan* duplicates the links made in Freud's comments to Fleiss, schematizing such women by associating witchcraft and hysteria. Christensen's work, as we will shortly demonstrate, was deeply (if idiosyncratically) informed by a range of psychological, neurological, psychoanalytic contexts out of which Freud worked.

---

constructions of positivism and empiricism owe to the mechanisms of repression. For an analysis of the paradox of Freud's relation to science, "sabotaging the language of science while claiming it as one's own," see Paul-Laurent Assoun, *Introduction à l'épistémologie freudienne* (Paris: Payot 1981). On Lacanian epistemology, see Alexandre Leupin, "Lacan: une nouvelle théorie de la connaissance," *Squiggle* (2006): http://www.squiggle.be. The epistemological implications of psychoanalytic accounts of the "event," specifically the traumatic event, have been particularly controversial, as evinced in the charge made most famously by Jeffrey Masson that in moving from a "seduction" theory to a theory of infantile sexuality, Freud "suppressed" the truth about the childhood sexual abuse suffered by his analysands. On this point, see Jeffry Mouissaieff Masson, *The Assault on Truth: Freud's Suppression of the Seduction Theory* (New York: Farrar, Strauss, and Giroux, 1984). Both analysts and theorists have taken on Masson's critique, though many believe his analysis of Freud's motivation to be fundamentally wrong. For them the central controversy concerns the status of fantasy in psychoanalytic theory and the relation of fantasy to questions of truth: for Freud, Lacan, and others fantasy remains an important source of information and knowledge regardless of its relation to historical fact. Recently, the problem of fantasy and the "historical event" has been revisited within trauma theory. For an important, if not entirely satisfying account of this problem and the relevant debates, see Ruth Leys, *Trauma: A Genealogy* (Chicago: University of Chicago Press, 2000).

There are other historical features to the convergence of the witch and the hysteric. Historians have also read Freud's interest in the medieval witch as part of the project through which psychoanalysis understood itself to be offering a radical alternative to institutional religion. William McGrath links Freud's account of the history of witches to his distrust of clericalism, a disposition which grew during his years with Charcot at Salpêtrière Hospital in fin de siècle republican France. For McGrath, Freud's reconsideration of the testimony of witches mirrors the anti-clerical politics of the French medical establishment (including Charcot) at the time: "Freud found in Charcot a modern-day defender of the tradition of men like Weier . . . a liberator, a view perhaps enhanced because it was set against the background of Charcot's great interest in the medieval."[53]

Freud certainly shares in the anticlericalism of the French medical establishment; and his record on the question of gender is controversial. To the degree that Freud's medievalism produced the hysteric as evidence to be analyzed, his theory encodes the "inquisitorial techniques" that Biddick ascribes to later historians and ethnographers. One could argue that the perception of the witch as hysteric (as a victim of both society and a disordered interior) played a role in occluding for contemporary historians the possible (albeit limited) agency an individual might obtain in adopting and negotiating the identity of the witch.

Filmmaker Christensen was, as we shall see, similarly influenced by the "alliance between psychiatry and anticlerical politics" that developed in late 19th-century France—a time when secular intellectuals and politicians like Desire Magloire Bourneville, or pioneers in the development of psychiatry like Jean Charcot sought to "laicize the public hospitals" by combining "scholarship [that] sought to

---

[53] William J. McGrath, *Freud's Discovery of Psychoanalysis: The Politics of Hysteria* (Ithaca: Cornell University Press, 1986), 157.

show that medieval Catholic religious beliefs were based on misunderstood hysterical phenomena" and "politics [that] invoked the name of modern science to wrest control of the hospitals from the church."[54] The major thrust of the ideological narratives of anticlerical politicians and scientists is to effect a clear separation of church from science/medicine by employing tropes of Dark Age, Catholic superstition so as to promote its difference from a rational secular modernity.

Furthermore, while the identification of witchcraft as, in Freud's words, a "medieval theory of possession" may have been prompted by the politics of anti-clericalism in the early 20th century, its meaning carries well beyond those concerns. Freud's and Christensen's medievalisms have had different afterlives; yet both turn to the medieval history of witches to press upon crucial epistemological questions of knowledge and truth, of power and desire, of punishment, and perversion. And the medievalism of Christensen's film *Häxan* makes this crisis explicitly a cross-period problem. It is to this film that we turn.

---

[54] McGrath, *Freud's Discovery of Psychoanalysis*, 157.

↷— 4: WITCH, PAST AND FUTURE
THE POLITICS OF RETROACTIVE DIAGNOSIS

As a film, *Häxan* stages a use of the past that sediments early modern anxieties about witchcraft even as it traffics, for much of its running time, in a sense of awed "medieval" wonder over the figure of the witch. One explanation comes from setting the film within its immediate cultural context, briefly described in the preceding section. To summarize this context: in the late 19th- and early 20th-century Europe, particularly in France, religious authorities and secular scientists were engaged in a bitter struggle for control of important social and political institutions, the hospital among them. One popular tactic for discrediting the position of the church—particularly of the powerful Catholic Church—was to link it to regressive notions of "the medieval," and thereby cast it as a primitive and retrograde bastion of superstition to be contrasted with the "rational" and "enlightened" work of modern science and medicine.

Thus, an "alliance between psychiatry and anticlerical politics" developed in the late 19th century, epitomized by the works and practices of figures like Bourneville and Charcot, as well as those of Charcot's student, Freud. Benjamin Christensen was clearly familiar with many of these men's works.[55] The bibliography drawn up to document the director's background reading for *Häxan* offers evidence that he was well-versed not only with medieval and early modern texts about witches and witch trials, particularly *Malleus Maleficarum*, but with the scholarship of the scientists and polemicists surrounding Charcot. Included in Christensen's extensive bibliography on the subject (a bibliography duplicated and distributed to the film's first-run audiences) are Bourneville's *Bibliotheque diabolique* and Charcot's *Les demoniques dans l'art* (with Paul Richer) and *Nouvelle iconographie de la Salpêtrière, clinique des maladies du systeme nerveux* (with Richer, Georges Gilles de la Tourette, and Albert Lordes). Studies authored by certain followers of Charcot, drawing upon various religious works from the fifteenth and sixteenth centuries—texts that purport to offer scientific "modern" and "progressive" theories about women's mental problems, especially hysteria—are also included.[56]

Given these influences, it is not surprising that Christensen constructs his film not as an account of the late 19th-century and early 20th-century struggles between Catholic authorities and secular psychiatric doctors, but as an account of history whereby a monstrous medieval religiosity is superseded by a putatively more benevolent and modern scientific rationality. As with the anticlerical campaigns of its time, *Häxan* ignores the religious polemics driving the early modern clerical debates over witchcraft, to say nothing of the culpability of early modern Protestant clerics in conducting mass witch hunts. With only one or two intertitle allusions to the Renaissance, the film insists upon a strictly medieval context for its often grotesque and horrifying representation of clerical witch hunting. This has the

---

[55] McGrath, *Freud's Discovery of Psychoanalysis*, 156.
[56] "Biblioteque Diabolique," special DVD feature, in *Häxan*, dir. Benjamin Christensen (Svensk Filmindustri, 1922), Criterion Collection DVD (2001).

effect of associating mistreatment of women with a "medieval" Catholic Church. Christensen, like Bourneville and other anticlerical campaigners, reinforces the image of that Church as a regressive and medieval space, one that stands in distinction to the apparently more progressive architectures of modern science and medicine. To be sure, the repressed modern Church returns, specifically via a brief mention of the "pious" organizations that continue to care for poor old women in the twentieth century, and, again, in a two-shot comparison of a mad nun with a bourgeois female hysteric, a point to which we will return. Yet primarily in *Häxan,* medieval religion occupies a dark and sinister space; it shares this disturbing location with the women persecuted by Inquisitorial Friars and other religious figures. Moreover, Catholic nuns finally feature in the film's Charcot-inspired "retroactive diagnosis" whereby religious women who believed they were possessed by the devil are presented, in fact, as nothing more (or less) than hysterics.

While the major thrust of the ideological narratives of anticlerical politicians and scientists—and of *Häxan* —is to effect a clear separation between religion and medicine by employing a conventional contrast between a religious superstition from the Dark Ages of Europe with a secular and rational modernity, the medievalism of these narratives is often a good deal more complicated than this overarching narrative suggests. For one thing, considering scientific work on women and hysteria as extrapolations from—as well as advances upon—the conclusions of religious men regarding women and demonic possession establishes certain shared points of interest, if not agreement, between modern doctors and medieval clergymen. From the evidence of *Häxan,* both groups of men appear to agree that there is something very wrong with many women. By and large, and following the lead of modern men of science and medicine, *Häxan* implicitly suggests that the Church was on to something in its suspicions that certain women posed dangers and threats to themselves and to society at large.

Yet *Häxan* also suggests that medieval witch hunters erred in casting their net too widely. The medieval men of religion represented in the film seem unable to distinguish genuinely disturbed women from poor women, more disturbing than disturbed, and feared by both their accusers and by the religious men who interrogate them. The film depicts several old, poor women as well as a few young, attractive women with no apparent connection to diabolism being taken into custody and tortured for the misfortunes of their socio-economic status, or on account of their unfortunate position as the object of male lust. In this way, the film, like the medical profession of its time, considers the modern man of science as a better informed, and more discriminating authority figure than their medieval, religious forebears. This association also forges a compelling and largely positive connection with the prestige and authority of the medieval clergymen while, at the same time, representing the modern men of science and medicine as sophisticated, humane—in fact, epistemologically and ethically superior to the "medieval" Catholic clergy. This, we should note, structures a specifically *male* version of historical progress. The progress made by the male authority through time, however, requires the disturbed "victim," now "patient," to remain essentially, invariably disturbed, even monstrous, across time: the figure of the troubling woman remains, her disorder always requiring intervention by the male expert.

After an opening chapter of quasi-documentary material on the history of witchcraft—which generally uses sixteenth and seventeenth-century woodcuts, drawings, and other artwork to illustrate a long archaic history—*Häxan's* second chapter stages a series of episodes that, cumulatively, encapsulate complex continuities and discontinuities between the two eras. The first section of Chapter 2 shows a day in the life of medieval "sorceress" Karna and her fe-male assistant. We watch the two witches spike a curative "brew" with the finger of a hanged thief, and concoct a potion made from cat feces and doves' hearts. The two sorceresses are clearly coded as both monstrous and gro-tesque: Karna's hovel is decorated with the skeletons of small animals and skulls. A woman arrives and asks for a love potion to use on her employer, "a pious man of the church." As Karna describes the power of her potions, the screen cuts to two scenes of the woman's erotic fantasies in which we see her in compromising positions with a ton-sured, and apparently lascivious, monk. The woman buys a potion and leaves.

The very next episode depicts two young men whose sci-entific curiosity leads them to steal a woman's dead body to use in medical experimentation. Renegade scientists, yet pious nonetheless, they pray for forgiveness, and an inter-title assures us of their humanitarian motives: "It is not from untimely curiosity that we so boldly sin," the title reads, "but so that the cause of many terrible diseases might be revealed to us." The two medical men are caught by a female onlooker in the act, just as they move to cut open the cadaver in the dimly lit room; she denounces them, running through the streets shouting, "The peace of the cemetery has been desecrated by two witches." Hers is a decidedly "medieval" reaction, the narrative intertitle informs us, at a time "when witchcraft and the Devil's work were sought everywhere. And that is why unusual things were believed to be true."[57]

What is particularly striking about these two episodes is Christensen's juxtaposition of witches and black magic with shots of early men of medicine. Like the two old women, these young men are up to unusual things; they

[57] This and all subsequent intertitle citations are taken from the 2001 Criterion Collection DVD of *Häxan*.

are, on that account, open to charges of witchcraft. Karna's activities seem to be somehow connected with those of the nascent men of science. After all, the mise-en-scène for both sequences is filled with shadows and pools of light— and dead bodies employed to curative ends (the disembodied finger; the corpse robbed from the grave) are central to the work of each. Yet if the film crafts a (weak) comparison between these two pairs of sorcerers, such a comparison is ultimately undercut by the stronger contrast also at issue in the two juxtaposed episodes: the two sorceresses and the young men will all be accused of witchcraft and persecuted by the Catholic church; yet the two young men of medicine, in contrast to the women, seem engaged in an activity that is heroic and visionary. For one thing, the old female sorceress and her assistant gleefully engage in behavior that is both illicit and stereotypically superstitious: the brew they concoct is a love-potion, made with cat feces, pieces of frog, and snake, all designed to sell to the foolish woman who fantasizes about her Catholic monk. They are not represented as cooking up some curative medicine, nor, in this instance, as experimenting with a medicinal compound that might relieve the suffering of the infirm. The two young men, in contrast, seem clearly on a search for knowledge that will provide a host of good things. Furthermore (and in marked contrast to Karna and her assistant's help in the seduction of a member of the clergy) the two men seem devout, praying to be forgiven for the "sin" of their scientific curiosity just before they cut into the cadaver. In this way, these two men are positioned *between* the religious authorities that persecute them and the sorceresses deploying "medicine" in the service of illicit sexual ambitions. They cannot be directly mapped onto either, yet they share attributes with both. Karna's work, on the other hand, is clearly marked as illicit and superstitious, signaled as a monstrosity converging on the grotesque. Seeking "witchcraft" or the "devil's work" here, as the intertitle puts it, seems understandable. Mistaking the nascent scientific method of the two young men for witch-craft, however, is clearly more seriously problematic, and the episode thus makes clear the excesses of a Catholic superstition also spoken by a woman (the female neighbor), one that is not entirely unlike the superstition of Karna. It also suggests something about the gender of desire: black magic women desire sex; their male counterparts are after science.

In this complicated juxtaposition, then, *Häxan* raises some sympathy for the accused, suggesting that the Catholic Church wrongfully condemned the young men for their medical experiments. Yet while we can see the Church's crackdown on black magic women like Karna as overzealous (they seem harmless oddities more than menacing monsters), their activity is, like that of the alarmed female neighbor, coded as superstitiously (even humorously) excessive. And the woman customer is similarly represented in humorously excessive terms: the black magic elixir works only too well when her gluttonous monastic employer, greedily gulping the potion, immediately chases her around the squalid dinner table, ready for his luscious dessert. The scene is played for laughs, with the lascivious monk in full caricature: corpulent, tonsured, and gluttonous.

This contrasting juxtaposition of the monstrous medieval work of Karna with the forward-looking scientific experiments of the medical body snatchers becomes clearer in view of the film's final chapter. Here, some 60 minutes later, Christensen returns to the shot of Karna and her customer (the woman who bought the love potion), crosscutting the scene with what seems to be its modern analogue in a brief set of shots of the modern sorceress: a woman of the 1920s reading tarot cards; another pores over a crystal ball before her female customer. Some things, apparently, never change. *Häxan* would have us see that many so-called modern women are still in the thrall of archaic black magic and superstition. And this is set explicitly in contrast with most men—particularly the director who interpolates himself as historian and documentary filmmaker, and the psychiatrist he presents later in the episode. These knowledgeable men stand apart from medieval spaces, ready to observe, explain, and diagnose them.

Häxan, thus, and on its face, positions its modern male knowers—doctors and documentary filmmakers—as epistemologically secure. They seem confident in their superior method and diagnosis, and their treatment of hysterics is largely presented as a great progressive advance upon a monstrous medieval superstition. And yet there is much more to *Häxan* and its representation of demonic possession than this view suggests. As with the work of Bourneville, Charcot, Freud, and others, *Häxan* also reveals a sustained fascination with the very medieval monstrosity it purports to overcome: wittingly or not, Christensen's lurid representations of the devil, of "monstrous" medieval witches and their clerical interrogators, make clear that his film is not a simple celebration of modern objectivity and progress. As Casper Tybjerg puts it, *Häxan*'s central idea, "that the belief in witches and demons was simply delusional is somewhat undercut by the extraordinary vividness with which Christensen makes the supernatural come to life."[58] As we see in the next section, Christensen's own delighted fascination with witches and devils complicates the claims that modern, scientific, male knowers are ever fully outside these medieval, monstrous, and epistemologically unstable spaces.

---

[58] Casper Tybjerg, "Images of the Master," in *Benjamin Christensen: An International Dane*, ed. Jette Jensen (New York: The Danish Wave, 1999), 8–21.

In a short introduction to the 1941 re-release of *Häxan*, Christensen addresses the viewer wearing what looks like a white laboratory coat and standing in a room that appears to combine a film set, a doctor's office, and a classroom. The director discusses *Häxan* as a film that documents "pictures from the Middle Ages" ("a dark and unenlightened age, both spiritually and intellectually") with a particular focus on the barbaric treatment of witches by clerical inquisitors. "Doctor"/director Christensen then offers his own taxonomy of medieval witches, four categories described to us in the manner of an ethnographer lecturing his students: there is the "professional," "the poor old women" (often with a physical disfigurement), "the hysterical woman," and the "average middle class woman" (who were, he states, wrongfully and often willfully misidentified as witches). Christensen's lecture, alongside his obvious disdain for what he would have us see as a barbarous medieval religious superstition, privileges the classificatory schemes identified with modern knowledge-systems. Through both his costuming and the mise-en-scène surrounding him, the director casts his introduction as informed by science, medicine, and modern learning. And he explicitly credits Charcot's work as the key to understanding "past mysteries" surrounding the one type of witch ("the hysterical woman"). He furthermore deploys discourses of science and medicine in a retroactive reading of the "professional" witch as a "common woman" with a "certain intelligence" and a "knowledge of the human body and the nervous system" that allowed her to make some effective "magic" potions and ointments. This interpretation leads Christensen to conclude that "not everything about magic is nonsense."

From this introduction, and from earlier interviews with him, it is clear that Christensen hopes his viewers will consider the film that follows as something other than a conventional work of fiction. He positions the film explicitly as non-fiction, and a work with considerable power to teach: Christensen likens the film to a "cultural history lecture in moving pictures" that "throw[s] light on the psychological causes of . . . witch trials." The director is thus simultaneously cast as historian of science, documentarian, and diagnostician.[59] But for all of Christensen's attempts to place himself and his film beyond the epistemological problems of "inquisitorial technologies" that tormented the witch hunters and their victims, the film betrays a confusion, an uncertainty, even an incoherence about the issues of knowledge and power circulated around the figure of the witch. In particular, Christensen's film can't quite clearly establish the borderline between fact and fantasy.

For example, in the re-release introduction, Christensen discusses silent films as themselves "dream" and "fantasy," before turning to make the case that his silent production, *Häxan,* nonetheless operates as a scientifically-informed (and quasi-documentary) account of the past. The confusion implied in this contradiction continues as Christensen immediately reveals that, despite the availability of sound technology at the time of the 1941 re-release, he chose not to add sound to *Häxan* because of a crucial problem: how to find an appropriate voice for the Devil? Providing a voice for the devil, he argues, could have compromised the

---

[59] Tyberg, "Images of the Master," 15.

film's status as a documented cultural history. The paradoxical suggestion here is that silent (image only) film—a media already linked to "dream" and "fantasy"—lends itself more easily to a realism, at least as far as the devil is concerned. Is this devil fantasy or not? Christensen's concern for presenting a credible devil—a figure that the film also frequently suggests to be the product of the superstition of the gullibly religious and the hysteria of so-called witches—betrays his own ambivalence not only about the putative "delusions" of religious primitives, but about the status of fantasy as a kind of knowledge best suited to silent film.

Fantasy and realism also combine in Christensen's own self-presentation. While presenting himself as the scientific documentarian in the 1941 introduction and in the modern sections of *Häxan*, Christensen also tells us that he "had the pleasure" of playing the role of the devil himself—and in this role he is featured prominently in the quasi-documentary sections that report women's supposedly hysterical, erotic delusions. By embodying the devil himself Christensen provides a doubled "optical device," precisely what he needs as filmmaker and historian: he becomes both the optical eye that guides the camera and the demonic figure at which the lens gazes. His demonic appearance visible on screen now enables a new and visually compelling history of *Witchcraft through the Ages*. Biddick, we recall, linked the visibility of the devil to a set of "inquisitorial technologies," arguing that, in early modern Europe, the devil operated as a kind of visualizing technique, one "that makes the inquisitor's [work] visible and therefore something that can be *counted as evidence*."[60] Christensen's film literalizes these "inquisitorial technologies," making his work as a filmmaker visible by occupying the role of the devil himself. With Biddick's analysis in

---

[60] Biddick, *The Shock of Medievalism*, 116–117; emphasis in original.

mind, we might say that *Häxan* is as much a striking en-
actment of *Malleus Maleficarum* as it is a documentary of a
history of medieval monstrosity displaced by the progressive breakthroughs of science and medicine. The objective,
scientific distance that the filmmaker claims via his per-
formance in the introductory lecture included with the
1941 re-release collapses into his own obvious delight in
casting himself as the demonic star of the show. Rarely has the
repressed returned with such élan.

Not surprisingly, the same boundary-blurring juxtaposition of dispassionate, scientific "fact" alongside spectacular
witchy monstrosities is also evident in the work of the
modern men of science and medicine, the "inquisitorial
technicians" who inspired and informed Christensen's
film. Under the guise of greater scientific and documentary
objectivity, for example, Charcot and his collaborators
photographed hundreds of physically and mentally afflict-
ed patients at Salpêtrière, and Christensen mimics these
clinical photos in the fourth chapter of his film. This section opens with a series of close-up shots displaying images clearly inspired by a belief in the documentary veracity
of the camera: an old woman with a humpback (who slow-
ly turns for the camera to reveal her hump); a woman's
head shaking with palsy; a woman with a missing eye and
scarred-over eye socket. The documentary film is understood to share in the evidentiary protocols of Charcot's
clinic. The lens of the camera, like the gaze of the doctor,
lingers over the figures in an apparent display of clinical
distance and objectivity. And the preceding intertitle proclaims the epistemological superiority of medical science,
as the title card opines that "during the witchcraft era"
poor, old women like these would be condemned as witches for the bodily "traits" they possess. This once again contrasts the cruel and humiliating treatment of poor, old
women by medieval clerics with the more humane treatment they receive at the hands of doctors and documentar-
ians. Yet only the intertitles work to convince us of this.

Taken on their own, these clinical shots of the four old women retain elements of the grotesque, the sensational, and the voyeuristic, elements found equally in Christensen's "medieval" representation of witches as in the illustrations collected by Bourneville and subsequently used not only by Charcot, but also by Christensen in the opening section of his film.

More than once in *Häxan*, then, Christensen betrays his position and perspective (and that of modern medical men with whom he identifies) as not entirely superior to those inquisitorial members of the medieval Catholic clergy that the film condemns. In fact, many reviewers and commentators at the time the film was released complained that Christensen's use of close ups to emphasize grotesque scenes of torture was tasteless, sensationalizing, and even insensitive.[61] The film was, on these accounts, banned in the United States and heavily censored elsewhere. It is not at all clear, however, the extent to which Christensen was consciously aware of the possible ironies of these stylistic and formal choices. Take, for instance, the striking juxtaposition of a psychiatric doctor's treatment of a hysteric and medieval clerical inquisitors' treatment of a woman accused of witchcraft in the final section of the film. A dissolve moves from a shot of a clerical judge looking on as his assistant uses a pointed prod to find numb spots on the naked back of a female as evidence of where the devil touched her, to a shot of a psychiatric doctor poking the back of his female patient looking for numb spots as verification of her hysterical disorder. Using a dissolve here encourages viewers to draw a strong comparison, as Charcot did earlier, between the medieval and the modern, at least in terms of the recurrent bodily affliction of the woman under examination and the methods used to detect it. But the appearance of a voyeuristic onlooker in the first shot—

---

[61] Casper Tyberg, DVD Commentary, *Häxan* (Criterion, 2001).

a figure who, crucially, has no apparent double in the second shot—signals a desire to sharply distinguish the work
of the psychiatric doctor from that of the clerical examiners. The doctor is thought to offer comfort, discretion, and
privacy for the woman he is examining, whereas the clerics
offer only aggressive public humiliation and exposure.

But consider this pair of shots more carefully: salacious
(and, perhaps, even sadistic) voyeurism is being encour-
aged in both, at least for certain male viewers. A naked
woman's back pricked by a man dominates both shots.
With no on-screen figure to foreground the male gaze, the
second shot attempts to efface the fact that as both exam-
iner and diagnostician, the modern psychiatric doctor's
position actually mimics the positions of the medieval ex-
aminer and judge. The male inquisitorial gaze becomes the
putatively objective gaze of the doctor, the documentarian,
and ultimately the viewer. This attempt to efface a problematic connection between the work of the doctor and
the work of the clerical inquisitors continues later in this
sequence. Leaving his patient (who has, we are shown, a
history of kleptomania) the doctor discusses the situation
with her mother. The intertitles inform us that the doctor
insists that the mother must admit her daughter to his
clinic lest the police become involved. During the conver-
sation between her mother and the doctors, shots are in-
tercut of the patient listening at the door and looking in-
creasingly distressed. An intertitle finally proclaims, "Poor
little hysterical witch. In the Middle Ages you were in
conflict with the church, now it is with the law." According to the language of the film, modern law enforcement
(not the medical establishment) has taken the place of the
medieval church as the controller and oppressor of wom-
en—the modern medical profession is set up here as both
an advance on the ways of the church and as the mediator
and savior of "poor little hysterical witch[es]." But by visualizing the doctor's examination in a manner that allows
for some of the same prurient voyeurism more spectacular-

ly on display in the shot of the medieval inquisition, and by representing the psychiatrist's tactics (the clinic or the police station) as somewhat coercive, Christensen, consciously or not, opens a space for reading this final section, if not the entire film, as suggesting that modern psychiatric medicine—and his own (quasi)-documentary filmmaking for that matter—repeat compellingly and disturbingly the methods of the (medieval) Catholic church from which it sought to distinguish itself.

This reading certainly stands in confused and conflicted relationship with earlier moments in the film. And yet it is reinforced by the film's final cross-cutting of two scenes, overlapping a shot of a wealthy woman stepping into a "mildly temperate shower" in a clinic with a shot of three witches being burned at the stake. If the film is unambiguously sure about the progressive sense of history it explicitly claims—a move from "the barbaric methods of medieval times" to the comforting and enlightened methods of modern medicine—then why are viewers left, finally, with the scene of witch burning? Why do the film's final moments regress diegetically from the modern to the medieval rather than progress from the medieval to the modern? And why does Christensen execute this move with a slow dissolve rather than a direct cut, which would more strikingly separate and juxtapose the two periods? The intertitles argue throughout for a progressive view of history, one that strictly separates the treatment of hysterics in the 1920s from that of witches in the medieval period. Like Christensen's decision to play the part of the devil himself, this final dissolve might be understood to mark the film's imaginary and visual unconscious, a subterranean current throughout the film, one that isn't entirely so sure that the present is all that progressive, particularly where the treatment of women is concerned.

There is, however, one further complication to even this reading of the film's contradictory representation of the modern treatment of women: the modern New Woman, represented in this film by the figure of the female pilot. The intertitle that introduces her notes, "The witch no longer flies away on her broom over rooftops." What follows is a shot of the aviator in front of her plane, waving happily to the camera, followed by a shot of her plane taking off. But which witch, exactly, is this pilot supposed to parallel? She is neither old nor poor, neither superstitious, nor delusional—nor does she possess the conventional, alluring feminine beauty that the film would have us believe could get a woman declared a witch. She seems to be a witch because she has usurped a traditionally male position of power; in this she might be understood as akin to Karna, whose "black magic" was juxtaposed to the activities of the young men making medical experiments early in the film. Complicating matters somewhat is the intertitle that follows the shots of the pilot: "But isn't superstition still rampant among us?" Perhaps the film *is* separating the modern, New Woman from the other women in this section, who are marked as superstitious and hysterical, and argues that rather than believing in witches who ride broomsticks, our more progressive age has women pilots who, with the aid of advanced technology, really can fly. Even so, "superstition is still rampant" among other women. However positive a reading of the New Woman this is, it also suggests the weakness of feminine things: the masculinized "modern" woman proves the one exception to her gender; she stands out among a group of superstitious, or hysterical females, women still trapped in a regressive "medieval" past.

Häxan, we remarked at the start of this essay, won't let its audiences go. Long after Freud's insight about the arresting nature of demonic sexual fantasies has been reevaluated; despite the compelling nuances of academic histories of the European witch craze; even as progressivist narratives of how superstition was out gunned by the wonder of science have been shaken up; *Häxan*'s attractions persist. Some of this is due, no doubt, to Christensen's experimental art: his ingenious special effects, his surreal visuals, his mixing of documentary form and fantastical fantasy.

But the fascinating figure of the monstrous medieval witch plays no small part in the film's enduring appeal. *Häxan* accounts for the Witch as well as her Inquisitor in a way that chimes with conventional accounts of the monstrous: a pre-modern "wonder" at demonic possession would later be presented as modern mental illness, pointing to an "error" in the diagnostic powers of the inquisitors regarding the mental states of the women victimized by them. Yet such is, in some ways, the smallest part of *Häxan*'s glamour. Such a progressivist account does not explain the striking continuities we have noted here between the post-medieval eras that we have touched upon in our examination of *Malleus Maleficarum*, psychoanalysis, and *Häxan*. These were times equally fascinated and troubled by the relation of fantasy to reality, more particularly by the epistemological question of whether to believe, and how to interpret, the stories women told about their experiences. Were the memories women recounted the result of fantasy delusions or real events? Both eras developed "inquisitorial technologies" that endeavored to resolve those doubts and answer those questions. In both periods, then, female subjects presented troublingly hard epistemological cases, challenging to the men in charge; female subjects emerge as the cases least able to be clearly and easily resolved through the evidentiary structures available, whether in the realms of religion or medicine. This view of the apparent "mystery" of woman is of course regrettably legible even in Freud. This is a gendered monstrous medieval as a particular kind of resistant temporality, where some women never change.

For all his interest in cutting-edge science or technological innovation in film, Christensen seems as preoccupied by historical repetition as he is committed to marking historical change. His emphasis upon the continuities between the female medieval witch and the modern hysteric—in contrast to the historical discontinuities between medieval religious men and modern men of science—places some females as the sign of a repetitive, if also fascinating, historical stasis. The essential state of the abnormal woman is unchanging. She is, in other words, outside history, while the men who treat her live through and produce the progress from which she benefits. From the perspective of the witch, the journey "from wonder to error"[62]—that is, from demonic possession to mental illness—has effected little; it has done nothing to change her essentially "monstrous" state, and little to change her abject status in society. Medieval or modern, the witch/

---

[62] Conventional historical accounts of monstrosity move "from wonder to error," to use Rosemary Thomson's elegant phrase (Thomson, "Introduction: From Wonder to Error," 1).

hysteric remains caught, disturbed, disturbing, and thus in need of rescue and rehabilitation.

She remains, internally, in an altered consciousness, gripped by a fascinating, and pleasurable "primitive" desire. A case can be made that Christensen's Monstrous Medieval Witch channels—for him, for us—a fascination with *not* changing, a desire not to relinquish the titillating dreams and fantasies, the pyromania or kleptomania, that lie before and beyond a well-ordered, obedient subjectivity. Theatrically excessive, audacious and bold, *Häxan*'s monstrous medievalism makes an utterly regressive, and mostly female, desire palpable, vivid, even psychedelic.

○— REFERENCES

Anderson, Gillian. "About the Music." In *Häxan* (Svensk Filmindustri, 1922), dir. Benjamin Christensen. Criterion Collection, 2001. DVD booklet.

Anglo, Sydney. "Evident Authority and Authoritative Evidence: The *Malleus Maleficarum*." In *The Damned Art: Essays in the Literature of Witchcraft*, ed. Sydney Anglo, 1–31. London: Routledge, 1977.

Assoun, Paul-Laruent. *Introduction à l'épistémologie freudienne*. Paris: Payot, 1981.

Bailey, Michael. "From Sorcery to Witchcraft: Clerical Conceptions of Magic in the Later Middle Ages." *Speculum* 74.4 (October 2001): 960–990.

Baxter, Christopher. "Unsystematic Psychopathology." In *The Damned Art*, ed. Anglo, 53–75. London: Routledge, 1977.

"Biblioteque Diabolique" [special DVD feature]. In *Haxän*, dir. Benjamin Christensen (Svensk Filmindustri, 1922). Criterion Collection, 2001). DVD.

Biddick, Kathleen. *The Shock of Medievalism*. Durham:

Duke University Press, 1998.

Bildhauer, Bettina and Robert Mills, eds. *The Monstrous Middle Ages*. Cardiff: University of Wales Press, 2003.

Bourne, Mark. "Häxan/Witchcraft Through the Ages: The Criterion Collection" [review]. *The DVD Journal* [n.d.]: http://www.dvdjournal.com/reviews/h/haxan_cc. shtml.

Bynum, Caroline Walker. "Wonder," *American Historical Review* 102.1 (Feb. 1997): 1–17.

Caciola, Nancy. *Discerning Spirits: Divine and Demonic Possession in the Middle Ages*. Ithaca: Cornell University Press, 2003.

Cameron, Euan. *Enchanted Europe: Superstition, Reason, and Religion, 1250-1750*. New York: Oxford University Press, 2011.

Cohen, Jeffrey Jerome. "Monster Culture (Seven Theses)," in *Monster Theory*, ed. Jeffrey Jerome Cohen, 3–25. Minneapolis: University of Minnesota Press, 1996.

Emery, Elizabeth. *Romancing the Cathedral: Gothic Architecture in Fin-de-Siècle French Culture*. Albany: SUNY Press, 2001.

Foucault, Michel. *Abnormal: Lectures at the College de France, 1974-1975*, eds. Valerio Marchetti and Antonella Salomini, trans. Graham Burchell. New York: Picador, 2003.

Freedman, Paul and Gabrielle Spiegel. "Medievalisms Old and New: The Rediscovery of Alterity in North American Medieval Studies." *American Historical Review* 103.3 (1998): 577–704.

Freud, Sigmund. "The Aetiology of Hysteria" (1896). In James Strachey, ed. and trans., *The Standard Edition of the Complete Psychological Works of Sigmund Freud*, Vol. 3: 189–221. London: Hogarth Press, 1962.

Freud, Sigmund. "New Introductory Lectures on Psycho-Analysis" (1933). In James Strachey, ed. and trans., *The Standard Edition of the Psychological Works of Sigmund Freud*, Vol. 22: 1–182. London: Hogarth Press, 1964.

John Ganim, *Medievalism and Orientalism: Three Essays on Literature, Architecture, and Cultural Identity*. New York: Palgrave, 2005.

Greenblatt, Stephen. *Marvelous Possessions: The Wonder of the New World*. Chicago: University of Chicago Press, 1991.

Häxan (Svensk Filmindustri, 1922), dir. Benjamin Christensen. Criterion Collection, 2001. DVD.

Ingham, Patricia Clare. "Contrapuntal Histories." In *Postcolonial Moves: Medieval Through Modern*, eds. Patricia Clare Ingham and Michelle R. Warren, 47–70. New York: Palgrave Macmillan, 2003.

Ingham, Patricia Clare. "In Contrayez Straunge: Colonial Relations, British Identity, and *Sir Gawain and the Green Knight*." *New Medieval Literatures* 4 (2001): 61–94.

Kramer, Heinrich and James Sprenger. *Malleus Maleficarum* (1486), ed. and trans. Montague Summers. Rpt. London: Dover Publications, 1971.

Lacan, Jacques. "On a Question Preliminary to Any Possible Treatment of Psychosis." In *Ecrits: A selection*, trans. Alan

Sheridan, 179–225. New York: W.W. Norton, 1977.

Leupin, Alexandre. "Lacan: Une Nouvelle Théorie de la Connaissance." *Squiggle* (2006): http://www.squiggle.be.

Leys, Ruth. *Trauma: A Genealogy*. Chicago: University of Chicago Press, 2000.

Lochrie, Karma. *Heterosyncrasies: Female Sexuality When Normal Wasn't*. Minneapolis: University of Minnesota Press, 2003.

McGrath, William J. *Freud's Discovery of Psychoanalysis: The Politics of Hysteria*. Ithaca: Cornell University Press, 1986.

Mackay, Christopher, ed. and trans. *The Hammer of Witches: A Complete Translation of the Malleus Maleficarium*. Cambridge, UK: Cambridge University Press, 2009.

Masson, Jeffrey Mouissaieff. *The Assault on Truth: Freud's Suppression of the Seduction Theory*. New York: Farrar, Strauss, and Giroux, 1984.

Masson, Jeffrey Mouissaieff, ed. and trans. *The Complete Letters of Sigmund Freud to Wilhelm Fliess, 1887*-1904. Cambridge, MA: Belknap Press, 1985.

Mittman, Asa Simon. "Introduction: The Impact of Monsters and Monster Studies." In *The Ashgate Research Companion to Monsters and the Monstrous*, eds. Asa Simon Mittman and Peter Dendle, 1–16. Farnham, UK: Ashgate, 2012.

Mittman, Asa Simon. *Maps and Monsters in the Middle Ages*. New York: Routledge, 2006.

"Pascendi Dominic Gregis." Encyclical of Pope Pius X on the Doctrines of the Modernists (1907): http://www.vatican.va/holy_father/pius_x/encyclicals/documents/hf-p-x_enc_19070908_pascendi-dominici-gregis _en.html

Stephens, Walter. "Witches Who Steal Penises: Impotence and Illusion in *Malleus Maleficarum*." *Journal of Medieval and Early Modern Studies* 28.3 (1998): 495–529.

Strohm, Paul. *Theory and the Premodern Text*. Minneapolis: University of Minnesota Press, 2000.

Swales, Peter J. "A Fascination with Witches: Medieval Tales of Torture Altered the Course of Psychoanalysis." *The Sciences* 22.8 (1982): 21–25.

Thomson, Rosemarie Garland. "Introduction: From Wonder to Error—A Genealogy of Freak Discourse in Modernity." In *Freakery: Cultural Spectacles of the Extraordinary Body*, ed. Rosemarie Garland Thomson, 1–19. New York: New York University Press, 1996.

Tyberg, Casper. "Commentary." In *Häxan* (1922; Svensk Filmindustri), dir. Benjamin Christensen. Criterion Collection, 2001. DVD.

Tybjerg, Casper. "Images of the Master." In *Benjamin Christensen: An International Dane*, ed. Jette Jensen, 8–21. New York: The Danish Wave, 1999.

Witches, Devils, and Doctors in the Renaissance: Johann Weyer, De Praestigiis Daemonum, ed. George Mora, trans. John Shea. Medieval and Renaissance Texts and Studies. Binghamton, NY: MRTS, 1991.

Zilboorg, Gregory. "The Medical Man and the Witch Towards the Close of the Sixteenth Century." *Bulletin of the New York Academy of Medicine* 11.10 (1935): 579–607.

W. dreams, like Phaedrus, of an army of thinker-friends, thinker-lovers. He dreams of a thought-army, a thought-pack, which would storm the philosophical Houses of Parliament. He dreams of Tartars from the philosophical steppes, of thought-barbarians, thought-outsiders. What distance would shine in their eyes!

~Lars Iyer

www.babelworkinggroup.org

Made in the USA
Monee, IL
16 November 2019